On First Looking

On First Looking

Edited by
Jean Kent, David Musgrave
& Carolyn Rickett

PUNCHER & WATTMANN

First published in 2018

Published by Puncher and Wattmann
PO Box 279
Waratah NSW 2298

http://www.puncherandwattmann.com
puncherandwattmann@bigpond.com

A catalogue record for this
book is available from the
National Library of Australia

ISBN 9781925780345

Cover design by Donna Pinter

Printed by Lightning Source International

*For Winifred Luben
and Professor Jane Fernandez*

and their heart for poetry

Preface

With a nod in homage to John Keats' poem, 'On First Looking into Chapman's Homer', this collection celebrates a long tradition of connections between writers. It is a unique showcase for work by new and mature poets, all of them united by poetry's gift of bringing us the world as if it has been looked at for the very first time.

—Jean Kent

Contents

Much have I travell'd in the realms of gold . . .
— John Keats, "On First Looking into Chapman's Homer"

Bike Ride

February 2017

Laughing and awkward, a tangle of limbs and pedals,
like the Argonauts.
And we're away.

Over tar and dirt and sand and obstacles,
past ink spills of calves on green canvas,
curious cows, heads barb-wire framed,
shivers of butterflies, dark and light,
endless white noise of sibilant cicadas,
blackberry tangles.

And then...
The bridge.
Hume and Hovell's way.

In the present we feel the past
like fingers stroking.

We lift our bikes up
and step into promises.

Moments

Written while travelling around Australia 2016-2017

Sometimes,
the surprise of sun-seared ochre
shocks senses.

Sometimes,
the whisper of ghost grey grass
suggests seductively.

Sometimes,
the rage of rock water
soothes steadily.

In the stark beauty of contrast
is the soul's solace;
the world's heart.

Rite of Passage

For my hard-working father, Howard Bruce Bazley.

He looks out into endless paddocks
— with no hope on horizon.
Seated in stillness
the pulsing beat of his heart in-sync with the
spinning wheels of the McCafferty's coach.

He feels the prick of tears escape him
as the herds of cattle melt into grains of sand.
A one-way ticket to Central Station.

With him is a beaten yellow push bike
the chain blight from neglect and
a grey duffle bag boldly inscribed with a permanent marker:
HOWARD.

The Sole

The soles of her feet tell a story.
They trail a path
that is forbidden.

The path is obscure.
It has windy turns and steep bends.
The stones attack from the ground like knives in defiance.

To travel this path, is to travel alone.
A journey with no assurance.

The soles of her feet tell a story.
Webbed in cracks
that will never heal.

Sugarcane Juice

...the same song in the hands / as in the mouth
Niall Campbell

She juices limes and lemons then turns
the mangle to crush the sugarcane. Her bangles
tinkle as she pounds cardamom and ginger,

then adds some mint and cloves. I can smell
the pinch of cinnamon she quickly mixes in
before she sieves the contents through a scrim.

Now with tongs she clinks some ice cubes
into a pitcher, rubs pink salt along its rim.
I watch the dance of her hands as she wipes

her tray of glasses clean; those thin, high
squeaks, like her voice, spruiking the juice,
calling us in. She's careful to pour every

glass full, she who makes us feel like nectar
birds arriving at her fragrant stand. The same
song in our mouths that was in her hands.

Cobra

This snake-charmer's less
a musician, more of a scribe
scrawling
his flute through the air—
no musical riffs
only an endless redoodling
of glyphs. I'd like to see
the snake breach type
break the loops
exact a new script
and imprint quick cursive
in the dirt—no longer
a stylus ratifying
its own capture
no longer transcribing
on every street corner
the man's cramped oeuvre.

Two excerpts from the poem sequence
Enfolded in the Wings of a Great Darkness

down the side path of the house
in a proliferating
parallel universe

the hydrangeas of the dead woman
emit their light
for some time yet

for some time yet
the light over her shoulder
falls across a wind-stilled pattern in water
that looks like a long
procession of doors we could almost
touch and pass through

a circling stream of faces

like a tree
rooted in the earth
that outlives us
how its branches lean
towards us
in the slight
3 p.m. breeze

the way
a young woman dips
one foot in water
and holds

her whole body
suspended from the other

and the corridors of water opening before her
shine
as if she were weightless

is it the light that emanates
from the dead

all this
we have no name for

*

out there
towards the exploding edges

the back-and-forth
dialogue of the blood
bone-cages the breath
makes its way
between

this voice
isn't us
it isn't not-us
it is through us

in harrowing circles
vast wheels spin
towards us

at the whirlwind's
still centre
cosmos-fragments
glitter

ourselves
stripped bare

enfolded in the wings
of a great darkness

A Winter Drive

Patchwork plains,
Verdant greens sit by grasses parched.
Seen from this ribbon of road
Smoky blue peaks frame the view.
Accents of wattle, brilliant citrus gold.

Step out,
And icy winds lure you to pools of sunny warmth,
So you linger to slowly let it seep through woolly layers.
Azure blue heavens complete the picture as we begin
To rise, over the Great Divide.
Rivers, flow, wide on either side

The summit ahead
Shrouded in dense pink cloud,
Pinked, by the swirl of dust blown from tilling soil.

Descending through cloud
The vast expanse delights our senses.
Lightly wooded either side
A favoured place where wildlife hide.

Giant gums hold firm steep gullies, elegantly,
And form a canopy above the winding road
The twists and turns restrain the endless road-rush down.

Speed subdued, gives wildlife time to hop away,
But short-legged wombat fail.
Forty-seven wombats, seventy-eight roos
On this scenic stretch,
All expired —
Road kill, on the Great Divide.

Down by the Old Swing Bridge

Down by the old swing bridge,
I jumped and played.
A check point recording my changes,
Like the pencil marks on a door frame.

Down by the old swing bridge,
Where lovers met, and travellers passed,
I dreamed and dared to imagine,
Terabithia and Narnia were fond friends.

Down by the old swing bridge,
The years rushed by.
I had grown like the weeds on the bank.

The fading paint and steady swing,
Creaking with age and worn footprints,
Framed the pebbled pathways
Where my feet skipped.

Leaning over the edge,
The reflection now changed,
Down by the old swing bridge.

Tea Leaves

The faded hues of autumn
crunch in my hand as they fall
and land against the bone white china.

The fated circle of life begins
as the leaves are dried, preserved.
They have been repurposed.

Rich memories of summer play in my mind.
Their rosy petals floating in the breeze;
now stained with life, ready for the next.

The heady scent of timely demise
wafts as hot water overflows
their flowery carcasses.

A warm embrace,
one last labour.
Now the sweet sting of death

.

Dog Meals

The dead women always fed me.
In their kitchens, water ran from brass taps,
next to the thick wooden chopping blocks
where the chinese cleavers lay glistening—

bowls of sliced pork belly braised in soy,
trembling with fat; plates of wok-seared rice
dry-fried to a near-crisp with onion and garlic;
cabbage, black fungus and beancurd skins

stewed with glass noodles and dried shrimp.
I have eaten of these willingly. The last woman
to die consumed three whole meals of the new
dog year before she lay her head down in the dark,

never to wake again to brew strong coffee
with condensed milk, to spread kaya on toast,
to crack open soft-boiled eggs. Nothing left but
a procession of black ants crawling across the counter.

Green Grief

I heard about your wedding in a Catholic church so much food and
wine live jazz band how you'd lost all that weight everyone so happy.
Revenge fantasies: you fell off a cliff got run over by a truck you were
buried up to your neck drizzled with honey and left for the ants your
plane went down over the Pacific you had a heart attack you were
shot in the eye. You see, poets have this thing for truth. The memory
of crying so hard I threw up but in the shower so you wouldn't hear
though there was no door on the bathroom. My therapist says I had
a choice I probably was the problem I couldn't be the woman who
would sit down and shut up or stand in a cupboard all day waiting until you got home and unlocked it. In my dream you were in my house
and my friend who is also a poet said I have to tell you to vacate the
premises because you would never ever acknowledge what you did to
me. Larkin said *Last year is dead* and to *Begin afresh, afresh, afresh.*
Repetition here is key.

*Note: The title, "Green Grief", is derived from the line 'Their greenness is a
kind of grief'; the italicised lines 'Last year is dead' and 'Begin afresh, afresh,
afresh' are from Philip Larkin's poem "The Trees".*

Grass Surfing

January 2004, Park Ridge, QLD

Tenacious fingers gripping
frayed tan ropes. Sweat
mixed with lawn grass—itching.
In the rear-view mirror, dad's smug
grin, as he accelerates harder.

Past the old mango tree, drifting,
free. Etchings of you and me.
And there up high, rusted nails,
where that plank used to be—
our throne, among long-legged spiders.

Dandelion weeds, fat and jagged,
whack as I go full speed around
the bend. Black ants fly,
like grasshoppers, out from beneath
my childhood chariot.

On Reading at Night

My eyes move in swift lines across the page, like Ghost
crabs scurrying to their damp sandy dwellings—avid to escape
the rising tide. They grasp the Times New Roman worms
and gnaw.

The midnight strike does not seem to faze them,
nor the battering of wind and rain.
They keep cozy in their warm
little caves.

For a brief moment I feel my control returning to me.
My eyes dart to dusty window panes, uninterested
in the worms that remain.

In one quick motion, my fingers find
the lamp's power source
and pull.

forgiving icarus

the feathers jacob
needed as he clenched
and broke struggle
the angel held chest-close
he knew nowhere else to find them

the seed of light icarus
dared pouring molten
wax on stolen plumage fingers stretched
just to brush the forbidden orb
he knew no other way to rise

the aspiration of mountains
zip-locked in wedge-tailed pinions
shooting arrows beyond
turbulence blown from the love of suns
she knows no other aim

what colour is a grey gum?

it depends; if it's just rained
salmon-pink gills gasp and stain
angophora-burnt
orange seepage

when summer's furnace has been lit
skin-fissure blister and buckle
curling sunburnt-saffron cleavage
around turmeric-latte inner thigh

if you are touch-close magenta-tinged
flecks of lichen-mottled
greens peel and clot
ghost-cream and burgundy cohen-cracks

(the one's in everything)
when the rain recedes it wants to fade
back to its bland name-sake;
drabs of grey disguise rusting sandstone

if attempting to capture its true
colours with boar-bristle it stabs
ochre-laced scarlet-ringed love-
notes onto your wash

Looks

(i)
At the Musée de Cluny
the carved face of a knight,
the sudden bones of his cheeks,
grave nose and the set of his mouth,
has you poised to kiss lips.
And just as you are falling
into the cold well of how he is laid out
the guard on the mezzanine
flutters to life,
a black angel,
admonishing loudly,
but with surprising tenderness,
excusez-moi, please Madame, don't touch.
It's not the only time
he'll say these words today.
He sees it all the time,
the way that lived life mingles—
past and present—seeks one another out.

(ii)
Days later at the Louvre
you're moved on from breast feeding
on uncomfortable leather pews,
surrounded by a hundred Madonnas
in just the same pose,
their calm faces in cahoots
as the patient guide explains
that milk will taint the canvasses.

And when you ask simply
but where will I feed my child
his eloquence evaporates
as milk, apparently, in air.
He looks from the Madonnas
to you, to the child
who is so astonishingly fair-haired,
blue eyed, all day
the French stop to touch him
and say *vous êtes Américain?*

English Woman at Palermo Cathedral

Her golden sandals
are of the orthopedic kind,
her skirt A-line,
some 70s brand,
her legs bare,
and her puffer jacket meager.
She wears her hair like a small child,
a straight fringe that perhaps she manages herself.
She carries two frail shopping bags
with patterns of stems or sprigs
and spends an inordinate time
with her camera phone
hovering over fishes and crabs
on the intaglioed floor.
This would be just her cup of tea,
along with Santa Rosalia,
the patron saint, one imagines,
of early immunology:
her skin here, her bones there,
the city saved, safe.
Our lady does not linger
in the side chapels and shadier recesses
of this space. She does not stray into the tombs
of the deified combatants of Mafia County
but stays in this crustaceous circle of light,
her sandals glowing,
her bags strangely still,
her gaze rapt by the smallest
and sweetest inconsequential creatures
of creation.

Parallax

My daily walk: the engine
Of muscle, tendon, bone begins to hum
On automatic pilot and proceed,
Quite empty of intention
But to enact itself at measured speed.
And looking out on this continuum

Of houses, gardens, streets,
Abstractedly surveying what is here,
The engine housed inside my skull turns over
And instantly competes,
Self-generating pictures—like that rover
Which roams the Martian soil and atmosphere,

Recording, sending back
Its images. But those that I devise
Are surely much less fact than works of art,
So quickly do they lack
All reference to their setting and depart
From what it prompts and offers to my eyes.

I can recall a droll
Advertisement that had the Martians hoist
Before the rover's lens screen after screen,
Across which it would scroll,
Filming a fake red desert, while unseen
Their high-rise city quietly rejoiced.

At times I half-suspect,
Walking the crafted streetscape, some such plot,
A suite of flimsy panels that enacts
That dubious effect
(The function of some small-scale parallax),
Sliding beside me, screening who knows what?

Unminded

No sign out here, too far away to notice:
The storm that sweeps the crest of the Pacific,
Wiping the atolls; or the mountain range

That marks the limit of the hermit kingdom
With sunblind flanks of snow; the Serengeti
Mapped by those stubborn herds again. No sign

Of drift along the faint meridians.
Less far afield the western slopes unfold
With almost faultless progress to the plains,

And nothing but some shadows on the Darling
Below a bridge to give a hint of it,
Losing themselves forgetfully downstream.

Closer to home those favoured destinations,
Happened upon, returned to, memorized
In anecdotes and snapshots, start to shed

Their dates and their occasions. Even now
The path around the bay grows dubious,
The lookout hesitates to name its view,

As some small tremor like a seismic tap
Slides under them. In scrupulous departments
The papers, or their virtual counterparts,

Are finalized and undersigned, the drawer
One folder lighter or the file reduced
Perhaps by some few dozen kilobytes.

The garden presses to the house, drawn in
By absence to the windows, as they stare
At rooms that seem to warp unsteadily

To hold their size and structure, unsustained
By acts repeated daily, or the force—
Imagine it—of an imagination.

For that, with all its filaments unravelled
And cells pulled with reluctance from the walls,
The kitchen bench, the bookshelves and the wardrobe,

Hung with its flaccid replicas, has been
Dismantled and removed and parcelled out
To others, for however long it lasts.

Broken / Beautiful

Schools of fish slide under me, a stingray
flicks up a mist of sand, a cormorant
breaks the surface, shakes his head and,

at the last second, all insouciance, slips under
the next breaking wave. I do too. Laboriously.
Seagulls speed past so low I fear my head's their target.

I've surfed with dolphins or they with me. It's not
unusual. Sometimes they're only two arm spans
to the side, so close you can see not only

the water-shedding, speeding shape but barnacles,
sores, chipped and broken fins, and though beautiful
it's unnerving when that much mammal

bursts from a wave. We know they talk to one another
but I swear they're laughing at our expense,
so slow, so cumbersome, so vulnerable we appear.

The music of time whips up the waves, whooshes
through canyons and corridors, through the shivering limbs
of trees. A strong wind, a fluky wind, it stalls,

trips onward in the space between 'should'
and 'is', makes of this present
a non-negotiable past, or rather a past

the future will fuss over, pick apart and
re-assign. We hanker after knowing

and are given change, the predictable, unpredictable

pattern of the genes, of culture, of the naked body
clambering from the sea and stumbling, flippered,
four-footed on the sand. 'Our love affair with the world

begins with a broken heart.' I hear this out of context
from a Unitarian minister. Is it true or just fine-sounding,
self-romanticising? Would you believe me if I told you

the world is beautiful and we will break its heart?

But it would be loathsome stiff

his brain filled with husks of books, culture —horrible!
E M Forster

Yesterday the sky was doing its indifferent thing,
grey on grey and all the shifting in between,
impossibly low. Suggestive. The weather report
had promised a clearing breeze and looking hard
it was just possible to discern. A colour chart
would have called the sky 'Shadowed Mist'
or 'Arctic Blue' but I'm trying not to be obsessed
with weather and the sky, I'm trying
to be relevant, to be hard-edged and clever,
to live up to my responsibilities and make sure
there's an ethical dimension to what I write.
It's hard. I'm like an alcoholic who is always
falling off the wagon, finding one more excuse.
This morning another fiery sunrise, the sky lit up,
clouds like upended sand dunes, their undersides
splattered pink and then the sun itself
(cue in the music if you wish), round and red
and blazing on the horizon. You can almost
imagine a prominence, that tongue of flame
shooting from the sun for a distance equal to
the vast homelessness between earth and the moon.
My books are full of birds and sunrise,
burnished light bouncing back from gravestones,
snub-nosed, screeching cockatoos, sparrows flitting
from angel head to angel wing, the inky cries
of slicked-back crows chopping at silence, more
much more. What can I do? It's where I live
between the cemetery and the ocean, looking forward

every morning to what the sky and sea
might have to offer; humble, helpless, hungry
for that first touch of warmth, the little shock of cold ...

Courage

On first looking
The sky
Like wet marble in motion, shifting in loops
Cracking
Bleeding around the edges –
Looks strangely
Like rehearsing for a meteorite shower

Against the growl of distant gods
Spitting
Belting
Pelting the earth
I watch erratic streaks of fury break
Splitting its own skin –

Then, a child, cradled across her mother's breast
Breaks free
Runs boldly into the storm
Hands raised, rounded – fist upon fist
moving
In a sequence of whirls and swirls
side-stepping, cross-stepping and reverse-turning
sliding across the wet earth –
dancing ... like
Moses in the storm
Wild and defiant and exultant –
Taming the sky's wrath

Was this —
Wonder or Caritas or Prayer?

And ... like an epiphany
The courage of the downtrodden comes to me!

Dew at Dawn

For Sophia

Gibran's Child
Like dew at dawn
Gathering the light
You came –
Gently –
Garnering your muse
Gifting –
an orb of memory
a pulse of pain
for the
People of Orphalese!

Reading Josephus

Once, reading Josephus,
I found this description of Christ: he was a black man,
very nearly black,
tarred with the Palestine sun
and shorter than most.
His hair was never cut. His nose beaked over,
farcically Jewish.

Hunch-backed
as well, a haversack
of gristle and meat
lugged about, pressing his spine down;
eyes tilting to the sand before him. Imagine that. Those
hefty wooden verbs
dragged out and thrown
before the listeners —
not sublime at all, not the easy construction of a man
nailed upright.

This was a lame Saviour,
glazed with sweat, heart pounding from the body's haul
up to Calvary,
where his tall disciples
and the squat metal guards
had to bend back their necks to see him
hammered out straight at last. Ascending,
with all the pretty angels.

Innes Foulcher (1897–1984)

The lace curtains in their living room
were like barbed wire, keeping the carpets from fading;
the furniture was sullied with a mineshaft light.

Everywhere, there were pictures of stiff-collared men
and crushed white women in bonnets,
cowled about the piano.

Nellie, her sister, lived by the piano
and died by it, never knowing the unstarched hearts of men,
fearing them, perhaps:

she would cycle in wool-heavy heat
with her skirt clinging to her calves, the clipped spinnakers of cloth
billowing, like a storm.

I can't recall colours there, in that Christian house.
But Innes took Christ and all the ranting prophets
out of this, led them

through the Pacific's wilderness
to Fiji, where she lived thirty years,
scalded with sun and work.

Some photos I've seen: Innes among the natives,
like a pillar of salt
or a sharp vein of quartz through their onyx bodies,

splendidly missed
when she returned for Eric, the mongoloid brother
Nellie couldn't cope with, alone.

I remember the early Christmases,
our visits after church, and Eric
with his grub-bellied tongue and lizard eyes.

We saw them always together: Nellie and Innes,
grey puffs of hair, and hands chattering with teacups,
words that hovered in the room

like blowflies.
How like coming out from underground it was,
running to the gate and the car beyond.

Innes out-lived them both,
moved to Bowden Brae, the retirement village,
with its coal-mine corridors and ceilings,

its assumption that age diminishes.
It was "modern", but she filled it with her old house,
chipped floral crockery

on the vinyl tablecloth.
From the window, the road stuttered between trees,
and the wind chanted

among the iron verandah rails;
ingots of sunlight were stacked by the bed
when, finally, she died, the last of the Foulcher girls.

How little we knew of her.
At the funeral, a vague succession of Foulchers
lined the front pews,

like milk bottles in a crate, each having a name
from somewhere in the Christmas conversations
of that dark house;

but, after the last prayers, five Fijians stood
and sang for her, all the island's flowers
opening, in their voices.

The Bowen Mango

for Jean Kent

One of us always plucked the seed
from the chopping board after our mother
skinned and sliced the mango and loaded
its flesh into her crystal bowl with other
tropical succulence, enough colour for all
of us. She'd be at the kitchen sink when

whoever scooped the prize carried it out
through the breakfast room with its wall
of small glass squares looking west into
Brisbane leaves and light, down the green
steps past the cluster of pawpaw trees grown
from tossed seed, to lean over the heap

of garden clippings in the yard, where I see
my older brother, who later enlisted to fight
in Vietnam. How he turned to me that day,
the seed's fibres sucked stiff near his lips,
his grin all larrikin, even with the trail of juice
trickling down the length of his arm.

All the Willing Hours

& we shall walk & talk in gardens all misty with rain
& never never grow so old again
Inscription, Wendy Whiteley's Garden, Sydney

Narrow paths centre the terraces through
fig and flame and bangalow palm; leaves jostle

the storeys with shape and shade and tint
any leaf will take. A sanctuary with roots

in her childhood; Lavender Bay her own
rampant alchemy to wander in, like a painting.

And for us too, picnic tables, a bell hanging
in meditation, a birdbath from a cast-out sink.

With her hair wrapped in folds of iris-blue,
Wendy tells how she replaced the debris among

the coral trees, cutting by cutting, plant
by plant and mulch, to revere them here:

her lover, their daughter. How all the willing
hours bloom unexpected grace from loss.

When Light Leaves Before Night

He sits at this table
with us
      without us

Once
instinct lifted the bowl,
steaming soup
down the right pipes

now he splutters
we stop
we watch

when he chokes we choke.

Baba feeds him
He's already eaten we say
… another spoon
Another

      where is the will?

she nurtures
it's all she's ever done
nothing will stop her
not even the wrong pipes

Once
he was first to sit
now he's last

      where is the impatience?

Once
his eyes waited for mine
winking when green met brown

now they freeze
hazy recognition
none at all
absorbed by worlds I can't see

      where is the light?

New car asleep in the garage
he always wanted a Mercedes

broken
English

Baba says
I drive you
like Prince Phillip
We smile—empty

      where is the pride?

places he should know
become places he knew

where is he?

a knife for a fork,
a fork for a spoon

When he chooses right
we can breathe.

is it you?

Too Young

You have boyfriend?
he'd ask

yes was wrong
—too young
no was wrong
—too old

I rolled my eyes,
wondered if I'd ever get it right

now
if he could speak
stand
if he could look back
what would he say?

would he turn to the aisle
watch me drift by in white
          mouth—*too young*—?
Or would he only smile
like the joke was finally finished.

Bars and straps
heave him into bed
I look on

Too young.
Too old.

... I understand what he always did
—you can be both at the same time.

The Same Cloth

the polish of the shops fades
the stirring of the soup slows
the bend to her knees stiffens

when he's not here
she's not either
—not all of her

... laughter
breezes onward
like it remembers to remain
by him
absent
and join him in silence

transient joy,
smiles stained by what was
and can never be again

the ache isn't his forgetting
it's our remembering

when he chokes
we remember when he didn't
when he mouths
we remember when he spoke
when he stares
we remember when he saw

do we wipe what we know too?
do we use the same cloth our Didi did
to wipe it all away?

—is that the only real cure?

Mango

I see
it sits in front of me,
thin tunic pulled tight like a woman
guarding exposed skin from an abrupt
intruder.

I touch
fingers trace its satin attire
the cashmere coat of oxidised gold
tickles the identifying grooves of my
fingertips.

I admire
colours flow loosely around its circumference,
colours of age and immaturity blend together in
stippled collaboration — oranges, yellows and greens
blended with a detailer brush placed into celestial hands.

I taste
divided flesh and raised cubes
torn from pelt by blunt teeth,
wayward nectar spills from cubed vessels
leaving adhesive trails down my chin.

Woman

Her backbone is like the spine of a book,
creases of skin fall in pleats bunched around the bound ridge.
Melanin, once even, now separates into clusters, like cocoa dusted
over alabaster sheets.

If you want to read
follow the veins separating stippled opacity
spread out from her centre
like roads maps to inner city scapes.

Admire her face — like skin textured marble —
fracturing harshly around her mouth, eyes and cheeks.
Watch as she fills each visible split with grout,
coats of varnish taming the ridges of her fraying canvas.

Touch her hands, feel her
fingers texturised by bleach erasing
the carefully ruled lines to leave mounds of rubber
in discarded piles.

If you still want read
part her covers and turn her rendered
pages until the tethers of her delicate spine
break.

Saddlebag

I carry it with me,
  not in a suitcase
  or a satchel,
  but in a saddlebag.

In this place
  I hear a horse's summer stride,
  the magpie's call,
  the crow's guffaw,
  the creek grown quiet.

I see eucalypts, red-tipped,
  and early wattle,
  and broad-leafed ironbark.

The grass is long and lush,
  or hard-bitten,
  frost-bitten.

In the gloaming
  chimney smoke rises over an iron roof,
  and I know that
  below the range grown dark
  there is a kettle on the stove
  and warmth
  and conversation
  and storytelling
  and love.

Make Another Planet

I asked God last night,
please God, I said, make another planet!
Another Earth.
With nobody on it. No people, I mean.
Let all else be the same,
the rivers, the forests, the mountains, the sea.
animals and birds, insects and slugs.
The initial concept was good.
Make it just for me.
I have the feeling that was a mistake,
but the thought persists
like an itch you keep scratching
even when you know
it does more harm.
Amen.

Snowing

To Jo — in memoriam

Snowing on the blossom, mournful in the clay
snowing through my winter, idle to depart
snowing while you glide and snowing while I pray
snowing from the anguish buried in my heart.

Snowing the departed, in velvety array
snowing Sundays weeping, lost between my Wednesdays
snowing from my soul and dark under your eye
snowing cemeteries, sobbing for your birthdays

Snowing on our love, a compromise amiss
snowing like a kiss that Judas meant for you
snowing when you fly, head down, to the abyss
snowing in my tears with sorrow from the blue

But the snowing ceases — blossoms will remain
on the icy landscape — craggy but content.
Like the winter-flake, my heart descends in vain —
yearning for your smile — suspended in lament.

Whale Fossil at Anatini, NZ

Time caught your great death
on an ocean floor I now walk
ruminating with cattle
and half curious tourists,
expecting more than this
smattering of bone fragments
beneath the understatement
of a simple glass shelter.
Remote from flesh memory,
you have become
slow limestone's image
developed in the chemicals
of geology's enduring darkroom.
Your elusive curves of bone
emerge now into shape,
sharpen my focus.

I press my autumn mouth to the cold glass
as if to breathe you back
but you would now be beached,
stranded in a wild south island field
where bony limestone outcrops
fret and worry with their giant grey skulls
like old men at their own wasting.
Better that you lie still
in the soft ignorance of rock
where I am left guessing
at the missing fragments
of a story we partially share.

There has been effort
in this little coincidence,
more than my short and easy walk
down a damp path
in soft morning's sunlight.
Mountains have been moved for this,
your great ocean sucked dry,
rock has been worn
grain by tiny grain
and you have risen up to meet me
as I have been lowered here to you
on my own fragile chain
forebear to progeny
unbroken through fire, ice and plague.
We are brought together
through time's momentous alchemy.
All points in our two brief lives
have been leading
to this tiny, quiet encounter.

Patient bones,
I will lay a small cairn of words
fashioned stone for cold stone
to mark my passing here
and our gentle, unerodable connection.

Worlds

i.m. Sandra Bernhardt

My English teacher ignited language.
Spare voiced, gentle in her large boned frame,
she came at the truths of learning slant.
I heard her before I heard of Socratic methods.
My teacher said everything
through the voices of those literary giants
who spoke with Biblical power
making room for new gods
in my young and eager self.
Everything only ever
through the greatest of voices
speaking forward from their pages
with such resonances
even in the silence
of our scholarly classroom.
I heard them ring out before me
so loudly that I hear them yet
echo and roll of voice and chant
reverberations widening,
gathering my tiny life briefly
 in a shared great span.

Eliot not with a bang but a whimper
Hopkins clinging here wretch
charged with the grandeur of God
Donne's love completing two hemispheres
a world in a room
dissolving doors and windows, lifting ceilings
words gathering to a little greatness

Shakespeare exposing the human
Hardy declaiming injustices
as old as Stonehenge
as new as youth
as vulnerable as trust.

Gentle, brilliant teacher
you placed me on the edge of an event
whose words open to me still and still.
You understood that the best words
had already been said better.
You gave them to me
knowing that I would carry them
like worlds in my heart.

.

From: A Modesty of Flowers *in nine syllables*

i. White Potato Vine

Social Climber. Sly fugitive, with
    the quiet desperation of those who
        live to escape their own tethers. The
small yolk-yellow rockets at the core
    of your launch-pads of pure white petals
        endure binding to the vine in ex-
            change for permission to climb. If you're
        thwarted by no support of pole or
            gate. Handcuffed at the wrists so you can't

negotiate rung by slow rung the
    monkey bars to the sky, you will turn
        inwards and contort into a thick
            basket of root and branch rancour. In
                that cankered nest grow no edible
                    tubers, just poisonous blossoms. Like
                that thug you most resemble, *Star of*
                    Bethlehem, whose bulbs hatch a hugger-
                mugger plot beneath forgotten soil.

Your star flowers would not guide three wise
    men towards a Christ-child through any
        sky's night. Still I delight in new-born
            armfuls of you, when all else in the
                garden lies frozen in state. You froth
wild above and beyond my vase's
        rim, like a consolation crown for
                a non-observant snow king, who has
                    missed the winter solstice yet again.

ii. Statice

Known as sea lavender, though there are
        no tidal juices rising in you.
Your blooms are funnelled tissue-dabs. Their
        hues dusty, as though passed through a bath
of beige-tinted face powder. In breeze
        your flowers rustle: white, mauve and smoke-
pink, their clusters clutching stalks that seem
        like frayed, praying-mantis legs. Your lance-
shaped leaves bring no more threat to air than

        a series of paper-cuts. If your
unique qualities were typed into
        'e-harmony', your perfect match would
be a bowl of *potpourri* left un-
        refreshed on a dressing table for
years. My dear, you are ever-lasting
        which is why no one can love you. The
plant who came back from the dead to find
        no audience for your story of

how to survive desiccation. We
        all eventually wither and die
but need no living reminders of
        just how that might go. Someone knows why
you were chosen to represent the
        loose-dentured, blue or pink homily
we all fear lies at the heart of us.
        You're Miss Havisham's wedding bouquet.
Our Lady of Dried-Up Hopes and Dreams.

Alcoves

Hallway alcoves
Empty spaces
Recessed places
for detritus

Death stalks these halls

Daily
Two days
Three

Close the doors

Hallway alcoves
Recessed places
Filled spaces
for garbage black bags

Garbage

Death dawdles
Dallies
Ebbs through passageways
lapping at life
final breaths

Keep breathing

You are my daughter-in-law?
No, your daughter

Oh

Shrugs

Gut-punch

Hallway alcoves
Transit spaces
Family gather
precious items

Three purple cloth bags and
a shabby brown suitcase

Decay

Two purple cloth bags and
three cardboard boxes
tied with string

Gone

Blank

Haunted hallway alcoves
Ghostly empty spaces
Haunted places

Ghostlike traces

Haunting

Ghosts linger

Keep breathing
Stop breathing
Stop soon

Keep breathing

Why?

Ella's Garden

A jet trail through
Summer night sky arcing
Lingering

Dusky sky forever
into space
hovering behind
Northern twilight

Enclosed by trees
three sentinel planes
guarding Ella's garden

A table on wheels a broom
A broken bench black
A cat (Anneke's)
sleeps as doves
coo

A crow flies low over
a green marble boat
(Anneke's)

Black darts
flutter fast and frantic
Flapping summer swallows
circle dive glide float
chipper chattering
are gone

Dripping roses and red gerani-
ums
(Anneke's)
Lobelias rosemary lavender
curving ferns

cascading and lush

An ashen pot
black (Anneke's)

Hydrangea and
pregnant pears

Being
in Ella's garden.

Ondaatje joy

The horizon sky does not stretch
but bends here
to encompass this place

It holds and enfolds

Protects

In a bubble of south pacific lapping
sometimes lashing

The breeze blowing briny
across my lips

Sometimes howling

Coral trees canopy me
shield as I meet
The Cinnamon Peeler
again

And remember
and smile
and know Ondaatje joy

I am happy

An Attitude of Waiters

Eyes down, they won't see you.
Though it's only moments since
they pounced, so that you're seated
now. And now it is the season.
Let's have them stiff starched,
creased to bow, tuned to any tongue.
Their world is pigeon swift, yet
priestly, they will stand like herons,
have had the special training.
Collectively they know each
other's signs. Once of the kingdom,
it is we seek their attention. This is
as arduous as prayer. Patience! Are
we virtuous? Sometimes we wave
the scripture at them. Kitchen will
have none of that. Even the specials
run out. Clock slogs. Appetite
makes monsters. It will pauperize
the soul. Cook knows how much
condiment. To pay's something like
Ragnarök. It matters little how
much silver you leave for them
on the plate. In heaven one imagines
them, crowded to whim, obsequious
of any peep. No greater delight in
their station but serve. Of course
you are already fed. Nor will the savour
ever lessen. Here on earth, we're all as
much for form. My model's Charlie

CHRISTOPHER (KIT) KELEN

Chaplin, with his two great buffet trays
and absolutely no intention to pay.
Cigar for after, that's the style.
And let the world cough up.

The Thieves Have Gone

Left less than traces. Bestowed a quality of absence,
invisible like fingerprints. 'Justice is an art of theft,'
Plato's Homer says. It took us time to know they'd been.
So many toys in the cupboard! It's negative theology.

You sense something, go on until you know they've gone
through the whole house. One can only imagine the frenzy
of greed. Is there even adrenalin? Police say that they
took their time. You're still really not sure what's missing.

Have to make a claim. The company knows that you'll
go on discovering things not there for years. And
not discovering. Some things you'll never know were
gone. This means that you had already moved on.

It's like that with the model aeroplanes mother threw out
because they gathered dust, then grit. How long until grief
came to them – and how long did that last? For years
the echo goes on this way – a death far off in the family.

Makes you wonder how it is to be raped, think what torture
is to survive. How little our losses we first-world-most
to whom more always comes. This little theft that stays
with you makes precious what you have. It's all so long

ago now, what's gone so inessential. Still you see them
gloating on, enjoying always what was yours. Makes you
think what it is to lose a country, to be banished, to escape
just with your skin. Now elsewhere of yourself, you must

make another meaning. Will you find welcome? You
don't forget. Every theft is with us. We are the past piled
up. You wonder about the country located right now
underfoot. It's personal, the passage of time, like

the colour of your language. You find yourself looking
sometimes suspiciously in the street. Is that someone
stranger playing old records? Does he/she wear my ring?
We know to be better than that however. First curse

forgiveness reconsiders. Can parties unknown be redeemed?
Anyway, the old theft's not so different from your own
packing up to go. What you've lost is just as you. It's only
the remembered missed. We're privileged with a choice in

such matters as — why come, why part, whether to return.
You see yourself sitting in the empty room, time vanished
here because you took it. Not far off the mystery's solved.
So all along and after all at least you were a thief too.

Southdown Estate

The sun filters through the trees
like spotlights onto a barren
stage. The trees whisper
like an impatient audience.
The dancing leaves are
ballerinas — delicate,
agile, brittle.

The trees that line the driveway
bow slightly like ushers
welcoming you to the show.
Or, is it shame that cause their
heads to bow?

The once stately home sinks
into the hillside,
a tired diva swallowed by her
chair. Cars rush by, their
whoosh mocking the
rampant applause — now a
muddy memory.

The season is over. Leaves
cast aside like flowers left to die.

The unkempt hedges
close the curtain.

Sunrise

Her head rises —
one peek, a wink,
the jealous clouds reach forward
grab her hair and

                    pull her back.

Next a hand —
she waves, says hello,
the bitter clouds scream like
banshees and

                  shove her back.

She runs

           jumps

                    leaps

Scarecrow fingers swipe and
miss.

With a giggle and a twirl
she darts upwards — a fairy
dousing the world in light.

Rue des Deux Ponts

From one end of Rue des Deux Ponts,
this is the view: the Eiffel Tower,
on the hour, doing its silver lamé shimmy.
In the distance, for five minutes, this shrug
against the winter dark. Then we're back to molten
honeycomb: trysts & tourist parties; picnics on cold stone.

One day in Rue des Deux Ponts, Ile St-Louis,
there's a patisserie. Heaven in the mouth:
mille feuilles; *opéra*; everything *chocolat*.
Next day, desire on the tongue — nothing left.
A black gap, violent as a tooth extracted.
Is it arson? An explosion in the oven? A bomb?

The workmen won't talk. Between the knife shop
and hole-in-the-wall for ice cream, they start again
from emptiness. It's common as history here.
Cafes, restaurants, little shops … winter guts them,
then remakes them with a new-old face.
In a certain light, even the Eiffel Tower is just rusty lace.

From this distance, from this street of two bridges,
the mending's simple: electricity in the night,
an insouciant sparkle against Time.
Before green buds begin on spiked trees, the sky
shrugs down stars. Every hour, on the hour,
a rusty old tower dances, diamanté, in the dark.

From 'Voices on the Paris Wind'
Sunday Kites

In the middle of the Sunday strollers,
while I'm pushing through wind which wants
to peel away my skin, I hear a boy calling:
"*Papa, Papa, regardes-moi!*"

He is slithering on his skateboard through the crowd,
gliding after the jubilant leap of his voice:
"*C'est ma première fois!*" It is his first time
for something — I don't know what —
but as he cuts a bright line through the afternoon
his voice cuts the fog around me too:

for the first time I hear words from this other world
rising as clearly as kites I can also haul down.
The string tingles my hands —

and just at that moment I look beside me and see
a small girl, almost bowled over by something falling
through the snap-freezing air. Stopped beside her father,
she peels from her cheek a leaf
like a yellow-orange flake
of fire — it is huge beside her head
and softly flapping, wrapping colours of heat
without malice over her crème-fraiche skin.

As if this leaf is a companion she has missed
all day, she greets it
tenderly — and safety-belts it
into the stroller she now feels too big to sit in.

At the traffic lights we stop: the girl, her father;
the boy, his father . . . the swirling wind-tossed Sunday
stills

around this warmth, waiting to be guarded home.

ANDY KISSANE

A Personal History of Joy

'…and once more saw the stars.' —Dante Alighieri

It hangs for a moment before your face—
a dandelion puff, a sheaf of smoke, wonder
before its vanishing, your exhaled breath hovering
above floodlit shadows, the lapping oval
which in winter, after heavy rain, resembles
the viscous crema on top of an espresso,
its aroma lifting, bitterness lingering on your tongue,
the caffeine hit like the exhilarating shock of an idea
that comes to you anywhere, at any time—
while digging in the vegetable patch, say,
feeling for the familiar globular solidity of a potato—
Otway Reds, glorious Dutch Creams, the pink blotches
of a King Edward that you've renamed 'Gough',
after Edward Gough Whitlam who believed in free
university education and the cultivation of all people,
no matter how much of a spud they appeared to be.

I love how we live in sensual, sensing bodies,
how when I spy the pied cormorant lurking
on the mangrove flat, then hear the flapping of wings
and look back to see that the bird has gone, I still
have a nanosecond of its presence in my head,
along with all kinds of ephemera: how as a teenager
I would dress up in my mother's stockings
because they were as close as I could get
to the scent of a woman; how diving under waves
I hear the endless rhapsody of the sea; how
walking in an angophora forest I can believe that trees
pass on their wisdom in ways we are just beginning

to understand. Recently, while roasting chicken thighs
with Jerusalem artichokes and banana shallots,
I discovered the miracle of the marinade—drowning
the pieces in a baste of olive oil, tarragon, thyme,
crushed pink peppercorns and saffron threads,
then tossing everything together until my hands
were stained yellow, the bowl a fragrant, rustic promise.

I suspect that the unmarinated life is not worth
living, that the neural pathways need to be lit
by all kinds of sources—the glow of a desk lamp
illuminating an open book, the sudden flashing
of fireflies intent on attracting a mate, the vivid streamers
of a city street captured by time-lapse photography.
In *River*, the grieving detective is visited, not by ghosts,
but by manifests who talk of the lives they once shared,
just as I glimpse my father sitting on the verandah
sipping a beer, or raising the lid of the barbeque
as the swirling smoke weaves around his outstretched arm.

If you are lucky there's a twist in the tale and everything
coheres, is graced with a meaning that never seemed
possible, so when you're swung in the tackle
and thrown face down into the mud, you lift
your head in time to see the ball spinning end over end
right over the man dressed in a white butcher's coat,
and even though thirty-five years have passed,
you can still remember how he glances in your direction
and greets your clumsy snap with a two-thumbed salute,
a perfect accompaniment to the endorphin light that swamps
your mind as you rise again into the shining world.

The Last Quarter

Ten points down at three-quarter time
and anything is possible. You fish
a brown paper bag out of your overcoat pocket
and hold it out for me. I reach for the apple
that is mine. When I bite into the crisp flesh
you say, "We need the first goal of the last quarter."
The intimacy that only barrackers share.
The joy of watching the lanky left-footer
storm through the centre square and let fly
from a long way out, the Sherrin sailing
straight over the goal umpire's head.

Visiting you in the nursing home, I want
to reclaim those Saturday afternoons,
but there's the arctic tremor in your hands,
your old bones that don't make enough
red blood cells, that only kick behinds,
the way you doze in the green armchair
even when we're winning. Somewhere
in my own marrow lies the moment
when you fathered me, that unacknowledged
gift—the siren finally sounding,
a horde of jubilant arms lifting, elation
sweeping through the crowded terraces.

263

I am handed her card like the ticket you get at a
raffle that says *you're next in line so this is what you get.*

263 is my number.

My clay heart wakens as my eyes trace her face,
her image etching itself into my malleable core.

She stands still —
and her little hand waving picks up the fettling knife and begins to
carve, scrape, pierce, form.

Another number takes life and grabs me by the throat
like a farmer lassos a wandering calf.

Five.
She is five.
My sister is five.

Please sponsor, waiting for 263 days.

The Koala

There he sits, mouth closed shut
two fluffy ears the colour of age

I wonder if he hears me

Beady eyes peer ahead
torn at the stitching they are weary

I wonder what he's seen

The Old Salt

He was a tall, cadaverous-looking man
With rheumy eyes and sunken cheeks
And long disjointed limbs
His old, hand-me-down clothes were
Bedraggled, mud-stained, ill-fitting
But still he exuded a sense of timeless wisdom

As a younger man he'd been to sea
Had sailed on barques and brigantines
Carracks, clippers and caravels
Sloops, schooners and snows
Knew the rigging of each like the veins
On the backs of his gnarly hands

Knew sheaves and fiddle-blocks
Stays, sprits and shrouds
Martingales and dolphin strikers
Could tie halyard hitches and bowline knots
And chain-splice sheets while balanced
One hundred feet above a pitching deck

He'd sailed round Cape Horn a dozen times or more
Seen men die – torn to pieces by flapping sails
And whipping clews
But could use a sailmakers' palm and needle
To mend a tattered sail or a shattered limb
As well as any shore-bound quack

RICHARD LANDER

The old salt - a scrimshander as a younger man
Carved elaborate designs in sperm whale teeth
And built 'impossible bottles' with safe-harboured craft
From scraps of wood, rope and sail to fill his leisure hours
Kept a journal in a spidery long-hand script
With sketches of his life aboard long-gone ships

But that was in the distant past
Ashore now - no use for skills he honed at sea
Yet still he hears the broiling briny main
And creaking timbers as they gently cork-screw through the waves
Smells the salty air and hears it whiffling through the rigging
The stays, shrouds, cross-jacks, bumkins, yards and spars

Nights are worst – now all alone
He misses the mateship of the crew
The gentle rocking of the lulling deck
The slap of waves against rounded bow
Old salt with rheumy eyes and sunken cheeks
Rudderless he sails on towards an unknown port

Remembering

Early mornings, dark as newsprint, I lie awake
Not unhappily. This quiet time is personal, special
Time to recall the past, plan the future, outline today
Thoughts seep through a rested mind like wild honey
Through a hessian bag,
Slowly, sweetly

Happy childhood days percolate like cocktail conversations
Sulky rides, polo-cross matches to watch
The heathery, horsey smell of my father's tweed coat
Pet dogs, guinea pigs, poddy lambs, abandoned joeys
Their names long forgotten but the joys they brought
Engraved in stone

Swimming in the muddy Murrumbidgee as it oiled its way
Between grey, grassless banks
The heartbreak of floods, bushfires, scorching droughts
Flystrike on the backsides of hardy Merinos
And plagues of grasshoppers, mice, rabbits
The stench of each is with me still

Life was simple then – box camera, air-rifle, push-bike, pocket-knife
My modest claims to a technological life
Living then was experiencing things, not getting them
We watched lambs, calves and foals being born
Knew that milk came from cows, eggs from chooks
Saw things die so that we might live

Dawn slowly disrupts my active mind like a whinging child
But thoughts of youth still float past like fluffy clouds
Half dreams of crushes, first kisses, dancing cheek-to-cheek
Writing letters expressing new-found feelings
The pangs and pains of a pimply stage
Now anaesthetised by the passage of time

I remember times when my body was lithe and free of pain
Could sprint and tackle, climb windmills with boyish ease
Ride the roughest horse, tame headstrong steers
Could love like Hemmingway, think like Einstein
In my morning reveries
I still can

Thoughts

Words no longer come as easily
Brain
Drained of things to say or write
Still
Like a leopard about to pounce
Coiled
Like an electric cable but
Unplugged

Once thoughts flowed like
Wine
Fine thoughts of men and deeds
Bridges
Of a Riverina childhood spent
Blissfully
With faithful sheep dogs, stockhands
Sunsets

Thoughts slowly filter through my mind like
Light
Bright thoughts then darkest shade
Komorebi
The Japanese call it. Sunlight filtering through
Leaves
A tenuous balance. Yin and yang
Equilibrium

World no longer that of my youth but growing
Madness
Badness. Things have changed. Gone

RICHARD LANDER

Downhill
Words no longer come as easily
Still
Perhaps this is best. I remain
Unplugged

The Shade

The sports star projects,
with his jokes, his élan,
the deep-city shadows of wastelands
where dossers trade lies.

Elegant Ladies' Day hats
send their mail
to the skeletons
coughing up change
in the underground booths.

The CEO's speech
spins a dark
that is deeper than language –

that hunts with the nightmare;

that celebrates pride, strength and fun;

that nestles like peace
in the untroubled eye of advantage.

Fallen Ash

Down here, weather is rumour.
As for direction: who knows?
There are only the tall and the fallen:
is that not enough? Once,
weather swirled through my branches.
Falling, I trailed cloud and glare.
Now, sky's healed back into leaf-net —
sunbeams, their eddying motes.
It will take me much longer
to loosen these membranes —
to slump, to relax into soil.
Not that before I fell earthwards
I wasn't, already, a lattice-and-vein city;
ant-crumble; trunk-lifted mulch . . .
My hollows will knit with fine rigging.
I shall turn into nest-wall,
be reconstituted as pulp.
I shall trail atoms, air by calm air.
My xylem will swell with the fibres of fungi.
Nights, I shall glow with their fruit.
Blue wrens will sing me as boundary;
devils sleep curled in my caves.
Orchids will rest on me, lightly;
saplings drive through me for sky.
I shall grow sunk,
and mangy with emerald,
deep beneath leaves' lightest rains.
I shall add the damp silence of loam
to the silence of shadow.

The ash tree referred to is the mountain ash (*eucalyptus regnans*) found in
Victoria and Tasmania. The devils are Tasmanian devils.

No more Sparta

There is no place for Spartans in Athens.

There is no place for the twitching synapses
Desperate to tear things up
Disembowel
Not in the civilised meeting space
Not with coffee and gluten free almond cakes
God no. There is space only for well-tailored cotton
Not bare flesh and clenched fists

The Spartan can no longer bite the cheek of the enemy
Not when they must sit and sit and sit on
The Committee for the Deconstruction of
the Art of Fighting Against Innumerable Odds
They must only bite their own lips
Drink their own blood.
And one's own blood tends to be unsustaining
It doesn't quench
There are no more weapons – just group emails
No wild dancing or simple sculptures
No more throwing each other to dust to feel your own strength
Just the click of digital bank paying digital bill

You know them by the bruises on their forearms,
The blood on their mouths
The occasion secretive flick of a hand that knocks
A glass from a table
To watch it break
The occasional foot outstretched to trip a
Vice-President of Essential Paperwork

The sometimes sudden leap from the low-ceilinged room
to avoid the compulsion to homicide
The now and then igniting of reminder notes
The flicker of a war in their eyes

There is no place for Spartans in Athens.
And there is no more Sparta

Blood Voice

My blood tells me I am supposed to be fighting
In long grass, in darkness, by fire light
I am supposed to be painted blue and screaming
Spurring on a snorting horse, unleashing a snarling dog

My blood reminds me that sitting very still will kill me
Freeze me up like tin men. The calm in stillness
has a smile that does not reach her eyes
Sitting still and lying prone – it hurts.

My blood whispers things at night
After decent hours and in the dark wind
In a language of consonants and bleeding tongues
It says to run. And keep my knife in my hand.

Kill it - it says.
Kill it with your nails and your pen.
Go to the beach in the rain, it says.
Stand on the edge of where you might just die.
Buy the shoes that let you kick,
Buy the knife that cuts both carrots and hearts.
Dance when you hear the drums
And jump if it gets too close behind you.
Jump.

Moment in Japan

Red, black and white
Koi carp in a pool
thick green moss
paving the sloping ground
granite rocks sparkling
in the sunlight
red maple leaves
falling softly
the red tide flowing
slowly
down the slope

do not hurry

please do not hurry.

Lichen on a Rock and Birdsong

I

It's an alienating feeling, being here
in a place not meant for you.
It's easy to feel like a trespasser,
intruding on a world not your own.

Alone, in fields of pale, pale green,
suspended in aural night, the pressure
of the silence bends and warps you,
moves you to be silent too.

Your breath is an aberration here,
your presence a blemish,
and so the soundless sky sands and
sculpts you like wave on rock.

Even colour is quietened. Bleached
emerald plants, a blood-drained hue,
spread in all directions beyond
even the most optimistic of eyes.

Scores of birds move like breath,
their wingbeats and song make the
slightest dent in the weighty stillness,
a touch like feathers on skin.

And the elephantine boulders that
adorn the heads of hills,
a kingly crown for each and all
of these wardens of the world,

their flesh is marked
by ascetic lichen, ever fasting
on the desolate, unyielding
skin of barren rock.

Press your ear to them and
hear the gravity holding them
so boldly, so nobly still,
sculpted across a scale beyond wit.

The weathered cracks and etches
carry a macrocosmic testament;
their countenance, an earthly vision
bearing witness to creation.

II

I have always commanded them
to speak their secrets,
(and I promise, extracting words
from stone is no more fruitful than blood)

but I see now my
arrogance had deafened me
to the words and teachings
they already professed.

I've never known claustrophobia,
but this crawling coldness,
the feeling of falling into open, open
earth, may just be its equal.

Melomania

For Lord Byron

O, celestial music,
Ignite this stagnant air;
The silks of sound, now woven,
A dance of wildfire fair.
The calls of countless instruments
and phantasmal tongues, your gift;
And in this stream of splendour,
you heal our hearts their rift.

For a painter may bleed on canvas
and a sculptor meld flesh and stone,
but your maker gave their heart to you,
their pulse to angelic tone.
And so, this song of heavens,
let it play, I say, let it play;
Let its colours trace divinity
and spark a soul from clay.

Utterance

for Frankie

after Tracy Ryan

The day you were born,
your great-uncle George,
ten years dead, cheerful,
round-faced, sallow,

slides behind your face
as you begin to fill it —
his a short phrase
your pursed uneven mouth

doesn't utter long.
                        Birth,
always a slow marriage
to someone's death.

The time your mother
took to shower clean,
that first clear morning
pressed and spread a vast

now that continues.
Your fast slowing heart
is retrieved from the worst
of terrors, and's held against mine,

your dark eyes aimless at first
and full of search.
We try to look at each other –
our gaze doesn't seem to fail.

At night, driving

After Derek Mahon

I bolt through in the night-wet Falcon
past the graveyards at Sandgate, street-
& traffic-lights buzzing away at the thin
soft rain lacquering the mangroves,
the windows and rooves alongside,
and past, then, the silent steelworks
shaken by geology, shares, demography,
resentful of what was there and of
what's there now, the change-over of shifts
gone to dusty statuary, the civic palms
in the forecourt there shed fluoro shade
across bare cement creased with grassy rails.
That smell of burning fuel and of asphalt
in summer's early arvos has extinguished
itself, maybe. Too much arson around.
That city's gone. It did itself in
with blunt forgetting, tunnelled
under and gouged away.
    When the sun
comes back, or the moon phases over,
waves offshore kiss and spray the outline
brilliantly, a patient weightless mist.
It'll only vanish and return, which is nothing.

A Fruitful Encounter

Barbed wire and high fences
suggest I may have stumbled
unknowingly into a world I do not intend to belong to.
Tent after tent after shanty after hut
meet with mud and murky water to reach
the tips of her toes —

I stoop down,
my pants dipping in the puddle behind
to meet her at eye level.

"Hello."
Silence.

I move to wipe the smear of mud off her cheek.
Recoiling frightened, she resists my gesture and
hurriedly steps back.
My hand retreats to my pocket – rummaging in a clandestine search
for
something, anything I can give — to show her
I mean no harm…

An orange.
Vibrant and juicy, it produces such a rich and sweet smell —
Her eyes widen.
I hold my citrus friendship out to her, my arm
extended as far as it can.

A cautious shuffle forwards.
One step, two step —

Swiftly she takes it, turns running and skipping
over muddy puddles to the
edge of the tents.

Holding it up to the light she tilts her head
from side to side as if trying to
learn its secret.

The Locket

He gave it to her
on her nineteenth birthday
gold-plated with ornate patterns
as intricate as a snowflake
under a microscope.

Inside, his portrait —
sepia moment, frozen still
that curl out of place
off-centre to his exacting part
soft, understanding eyes

In his hand, just visible —
his slouch hat with the glint
of the Rising Sun.

The photograph flipped —
in cursive, written
'Hazel, My Love'
lightly stained with
a dash of coffee.

Wrinkled hands clasp it tightly,
her fingers interlocking and
caressing lovingly
the outlines of his
familiar face.

Walking home at 5pm

The sunlight is heavy
and spreading

It sifts through leaves
to settle on my skin

A breeze fizzes the branches
scatters the yellowgold

Suddenly a shadow car cuts the road

Still the sunlight comes back
like a wave rolling in

The Cave

opens into a blackened roof, veined
and drying, and out of it issuing
sighs or rattles. So small, and yet
it dominates the room. Wetting now and then
with swabs does nothing to slow down
the shallowing breath, the chill creeping
in from the limbs. Through it all, her eyes
stay open, seeing everything and nothing.

Lines in Lviv, formerly Lvov, formerly Lemburg, near Limbo

The fine art of pretension, putting on airs
is exemplified by this, sitting in an outdoor cafe
on a chair tilting on cobblestones
watching the block-headed polity walk past,
hard starers every one of them,
cheerful and grim, indifferent to this sketching
which seems to slide easily into the sunlight
of a tree's blazing green head of hair
and the glowering sky, cool as a separation.
A clarinet, played well, breezes through the streets,
its notes as distinct and indistinct as turning inwards
once more, now the shouting in the square has died down
and the crowds are trudging back home, the earth relaxing
into its orbit once again. A dim sheen
rises now from the cobblestones as a pigeon inspects
each bump as thoroughly as a phrenologist.

It's like a giant family, being in a country
as monocultural, everyone a distant relation
except me. And that's fine.
I've examined myself in the mirror
and wouldn't dream of inflicting my relatedness
on anyone who didn't want it.
The telegraph wires are a nodal symphony
stretching across the street and sagging
into emptiness. Who wants to know about a poet
by his or her poetry? Wouldn't a blood test be easier,
or a DNA swab? Leave me out of it,
I'm just filling in time before I go.

Somatic Symptoms of Grief

Like falling neck deep into cement
(If only I'd fallen all the way in)
Was breathing always this hard?

A boa takes up residence around my neck,
constricting.

Why does this feeling comfort me?

The silhouette of a man runs for me,
his bruising blows force me to the ground.

Why is my surrender not enough?

A fog settles around me —
it enters my mouth and fills my blood.

Who am I?

The darkness hardens like iron inside;
I cannot move — so, I stay still.

Stillness brings calmness — right?

Then, my toes twitch.

The Poem Pisky

Movement in my periphery —
it darts behind the laundry hamper.
I fix my eyes and tiptoe toward it.
Gone.

With a flounce I settle back into my chair
waiting —
I hear thudding, feather-light feet.
With the speed of an asp my eyes strike.

Vanished, no trace.
Moving to the closet I fling open the doors.
The clothes whisper with the left over breeze.

A shadow blocks the light of the window.
With a galloped step I stand before it,
my glare trailing the frame.
Nothing.

Again settling into the chair I stare
at the bare page —
a poem hiding just beyond my grasp.

Stop.

We move too fast.

Time used to be endless and silent but
now impatient and ticking
we let the buzz of vibrating pockets
dictate our way, the bings and rings
of black glass insist hasten without delay

we guzzle our coffee still blistering hot
we drive the limit or push the needle
until it pricks us with the shrill of sirens
we walk blurred halls past fuzzy faces
just for the precious grindstone that leaves
grit on our nose

Stop.

Remember when the ticking slowed?

The warmth of coffee left out for a moment.
The crunch of fresh toast Sunday morning.

The sensation of a hot shower on cold skin.
The echo of bellbirds on a forest walk.

The soft rhythm of rain tracing windowpane.
Inhaling the savoury aroma of old book pages.

Butterfly kisses and delighted squeals from a child.
A lover's hands gliding over your skin.

We move too fast.

Reaching Aegina

for John Lucas

As your ferry nears the shore,
the hut-shaped haven on the wharf will reel you in
to the blue door and the bell tower looking out to sea.
It waits for you with all the self-possession of islands
held in its stance and hallowing curves:
the miniscule church of Saint Nicholas the Thalassinos,
the sailors' saint. And surely the children's favourite too —
those smooth white domes are
a double-header icecream held out to a child.

You approach with curiosity, even trust,
this beckoning to strangers,
this fishermen's welcome home.
Inside, it's a cosy cave with bright blue walls
sprinkled with flowers and circled by presences,
long-faced saints in rich dark colours backed by gold,
and St Nicholas centred to summon his sailors in.
So small and round and quiet a place,
it seems your very own.

Last time I was there, just off the early ferry,
a boy breezed in — eleven or twelve years old,
late for school and out of breath —
crossed himself, that easy intimate reflex,
and zipped around like
a skateboarder skimming a circuit,
reaching and touching here and there,
leaning to kiss an icon in fervent haste,
then just as suddenly made off
with a clank of the door and a call to a friend outside.

Was it a ritual to speed the day?
A careless penance maybe?
Silence at least seemed quietly pleased:
he'd made it of a piece, the space,
with all the patient faces of one mind.
Is there a word in Greek
for that quick grace, that butterfly touch
lighting and lifting? — most ordinary of things
and little enough to be remembered still.

Tough Muscle

I'd swear by you for a stout companion
reliably there in your dim room
just the other side of the wall
with your late-night muffled drum.
More sturdy than flighty lungs
more doughty than drudging gut
you are the faithful insomniac
and dragoman of dreams
a connoisseur of blood and joy and pain.
We take you for granted old Dobbin
red centre nub of love
till clogged balked worn out anguish-stabbed
some spasm murmurs dread.
Even then the heel of a palm
may mime you to restart
open to further persuasion's
intricate tinkering skill.
Strangest of all you can resume
your dance of time in a second breast.
Heart you have so much heart
and a mind of your own.
I'd say you're the first philosopher
pulse of the mother of Tao.
The merest hint of your shape and song
we recognize
O sweet Soweto beat.
I remember from years ago
an earthenware bowl of midnight purple
heartsease lifting my heart
with their twenty upright faces swaying
courage courage courage.

Hello

For my daughters

A rush,
a tsunami of love almost crushes me
I can't breathe
And then,
hello

Our eyes meet
I am yours, utterly, completely
You are mine

I don't want to move,
I can't
Anchored, my instincts are ignited
I inhale you
My eyes wide explore you,
every inch of you

You are here,
hello

I behold you
Be gone imagination, I no longer need you
You are here,
hello

An awakening,
my gut twists
I'm ready to lunge,
a lioness stirs

You twist, turn, seek me,
hello

Your scent is infused within me
Your sounds awaken every fibre of me
Will I ever sleep again?
I trust not
I care not
I am yours and you are mine

Another rush, that tidal crush
I'm here again, this time anew
I remember to breathe
And then,
hello

Our eyes meet
I am yours, utterly, completely
You are mine

You too are here,
hello

My heart bursts,
love boundless, limitless,
shared now by two

How I love you so,
hello

Thrift Store Rush

Newtown, Sydney.

There's nothing more comforting
than the scent of that room.
Indigo hues washed away
by drawn out summers and
the insistent testing of perfumes.

Knitted wools intermingle,
with memories past.
Each count of yarn stands,
as a woven survivor
of a hundred rigorous washes.

A hole cuts through the twill
of a kimono sweater,
the tack of thread pulling
at a quilted duffel layer.

But still, here I stand
a paragon of treasure
laying in my hands
in exchange for one or two
copper coins.

Bugger

He's curious.
With no roads as barriers,
or paths to discourage the stray

I watch as he walks,
drunken, without purpose.

But still,
the iridescent light
of my study room guides him

to a heavenly end
and it causes me to question:

Who is really living?

The human yielding to a
tattered textbook

or the precarious mosquito
on his daily escapade
to Edison's enlightenment.

CAROLYN RICKETT

Sweet Peas

for my parents

The green shoot will break through the rock ...
our tombs of loss will shatter, and there will be a
homecoming. There will. There will. There will.
—Lewis Packer

Every year your hands wire trellis to the sloping fence
staking out the hope of something more than grey.

Then with a watering can you form a nimbus cloud
and rain on seeds in drought-bound soil.

We wait not knowing when the awkward stalk who keeps
tight-lipped for weeks might have something to say.

And always, every year, the first flower calls us outside
to hear its perfumed mouth finally speaking colour.

Waking

for George, my father

Every Sunday morning—
the tune now belongs to childhood days—
my father's song would chip and
split the morning frost

>   *Oh give me a home where the buffalo roam*
>   *Where the deer and the antelope play ...*
>   *Where seldom is heard a discouraging word ...*

would wrap the weatherboard ice
in a slow combusting hymn
Then his steps—ahead of words—
would come unstuttered down the hall
to sing me to the fire's heart.

Seeing Deep

Life is a fine tapestry.
Looping together the magic with the tragic,
It is viewed from the inside out.
Plumbing life's meaning courts frustration,
While failing to focus on its sense is the art of fools.

Those we love are no less deep,
If we take a moment to explore.
She cannot be captured in a single snap,
Let alone a catalogue of images.
Nor is she fathomed in a lifetime of loving,
Although I come close.

Perhaps the One we call God is also much more;
More than our idols, our metaphors, our careful credos.
What if he is our mother,
And, she is our father?
What if God is larger and smaller,
Weaker and stronger,
Wilder and tamer,
Older and younger
Closer and farther,
One, and a few?
Maybe, if we chance a deeper glance,
We unearth a God who is greater than God.[1]

---

1 For this insight, I am indebted to Meister Eckhart who says "God is greater than God."

Summer

Summer is coming; the first hot days have already arrived
At the end of winter when spring is barely here.

Summer's bushfires sear the headlands
While winter's blizzards cloak the high mountains,
Fire hoses and snow ploughs
Struggle against nature in uneven battles.

Winter was dry, the daffodils were not happy.
Their yellow flowers stayed locked within their bulbs.

Wattles savour a dry winter,
Swathes of yellow blooms transform the bushland.
Lining the highways and climbing the hill sides.

Come spring; come winds to
Spread pollen from the wattle blossoms,
Spread smoke from burn-offs.
Fill eyes and lungs with pollen and smoke and ash.

Dry bushland is poised to ignite.
Be it from lightning strike or human hand.
Most of the city has escaped bushfires in recent years
Thanks to controlled burning.

When nature gets the upper hand
Fire takes control, despite our best efforts.

Small children anticipate summer with glee,
Old bones don't like the heat,
Old lungs can't breathe dusty air,
Old minds dread the menace of fire.
Summer.

R.E.M.

My electric fingertips slay the damn dream. Remembered fables
permute a stolen
aroma—

Like infested meat to the dogs, the stench greets me; a girl's broken
complexion: scorched hair,
drowned eyes;
I am already drowned, thus our eyes meet. Gasping for granite above
water, when cheeks
only receive:
Unruly sand, that changes within seconds at the dictatorship of the
wind's direction. I swallow
every grain—
It gnaws between my teeth. Becoming one with sand, I am now in-
control and make
a castle

Repeat

The Gardener's Heart

A moth, searches
your stomach
it eats the strings of fabric from the heart —

Flutter.

Flutter.

You strum
the string as your harp in the garden.
You've grown tired of its tune —

Twang.

Twang.

The string snaps
under your overbearing green-thumb
and tear drops form from the nylon —

Bleed.

Bleed.

The tears fall
off the shoulder onto
the sound box and feed the flowerbed —

Drip.

Drip.

The Pull and Yearn

On first looking this log
was an indiscriminate, banal log.
Like a snake detaching its skin
the bark, flaked away revealing the harshness of its hardness.

Moss enveloped the south side and critters
of all sizes and appendages titivated its presence.
It was hollow, much like
my last girlfriend's break-up excuse.

There was no discernible reason to be drawn to this log —
it was dreary. Not something I would usually notice
but from within the catacombs of my mind a faint
something, a recognition?

This log had connotations
I don't know what, but it was mine.

Vegemite

Sitting on the breakfast nook
an icon of a nation,
edible, spreadable
contained within a glassless vessel

Imagine what it could have been
an icon of the world,
edible, spreadable, incredible
but trapped in a glassless vessel

Could it have brought peace
to the nations that are at war?
edible, spreadable, incredible, halal-able
but still resides in a glassless vessel

And what of the future?
could it shape the way we live?
edible, spreadable, incredible, halal-able, sustainable
yet remains in its glassless vessel

And if it could break free
the glassless vessel no longer its home,
edible, spreadable, incredible, halal-able, sustainable,
uncontainable

Horse

Bending to the earth, the silhouette of a horse
is a hillside, dense as almond wood.
From wither to tail, a bristling escarpment
drops to a levelling range and a broadening flatland,
its bare-blank spine, cradles the sprawling horizon
and valley depths. At first light, with the long
slope of its neck plunging groundward,
it stands steaming among the outcrops,
thawing with the quartz stone earth.
As the sun lifts, the mist comes quietly,
idly avalanching the treetops before draining
into the white void of the morning air.
On ironed hooves and crooked stumps, the horse
stays grazing, dipping and disappearing into itself.
Frostmelt drips from the red-brown furrows of its hide
down into the mud and clover.
                              Blowing in from the tops,
the air shifts and stirs; long flanks of light
strip shadows from the clay. Dozy, not asleep,
the horse sinks further into a wilderness within its skull.
How easily it drifts, stooped under such tonnage,
poised and unmoved in its thickly furred slack frame.
Motionless, under half-closed lids it has slipped,
as if flown from the bars of an unlocked gate,
bolted to the blind spot between its eyes,
dawning headlong deep in the dew.

The Stick

1

It was a length of garden cane intended for growth,
a strip of bamboo, staked with ties to the soil.

Spring loaded with fixed intent, it could hoist
a flowering vine out of the tangles of knotted briar

and tame the midsummer creepers with its hard
unwavering line. Whip-like and limber,

unyielding as it had to be, it was an instrument
of my mother's affection, a measure of untold burden,

of tautened coil and twine, rooted in living memory
and dished out through the acts of labour and devotion.

It worked like a charm and I stared with frozen
watchfulness whenever she took it into her hand.

2

Then up and away we ran,
scattering in all directions,
bolting hell-for-leather
and running the gauntlet

through the halls of the house,
occasionally copping
razory slashes at the back
of the heels and knees,

before kicking back
and sticking our hands out,
while freeing the stiffened
key lock at the back of the door.

3

Once, when my mother was sleeping,
I took the stick into my own hands,
playing with its tension to see how far

it would bend. I laid it flat like a spirit level
and with all my boyhood strength
brought its top and tail ends down,

hoping that every shard of its tensile magic
would shatter from its glacial core.
I wanted to hear its threshold break,

to see each splintered half lying broken.
I wanted to turn it from a mother-child wand
into the image of an earthborn gift.

Soul Voice

Matriarch:
Whose strength echoes across the rocky outlined ridge,
       still, calm, thoughtful;
Whose faith sings along the valley,
       through the caverns and
       back towards the light;
Whose kindness whispers in the gloaming
       as the heart of the earth bruises;
Whose passion for learning laughs into the sun,
       warming the wide stretches of sky.
Mother.
Ma.
Matriarch.

Editors' Notes

'... into thanks, and silence in which
another voice may speak ... .'
— Mary Oliver, 'Thirst'

We offer colossal thanks again to Dr David Musgrave from Puncher & Wattmann who has been instrumental in the publication of this anthology. Appreciation and thanks goes to the Avondale College of Higher Education creative writing class for their enthusiasm and commitment in developing their work for this anthology; it has been a joy and inspiration working with them.

An enormous measure of gratitude is offered here to the established poets who generously contributed their voices and work to this year's anthology, and in so doing have enriched the quality and breadth of poetry on offer.

The cover design for this anthology represents the talented work of Donna Pinter, an artist and graphic design lecturer who teaches at Avondale College of Higher Education.

For her generous and expert assistance with the preparation of the anthology manuscript, we pay tribute to Margaret House.

We recognise again Professor Jane Fernandez, Professor Ray Roennfeldt, Associate Professor Paul Race, Tony Martin, Associate Professor Maria Northcote, and Associate Professor Daniel Reynaud for their ongoing support. And to the many well-wishers who have passed on their encouragement for publishing this anthology, your support of poetry remains paramount.

—Jean Kent and Dr Carolyn Rickett
August 2018

Biographical Notes

LYN BARDEN is a Senior English teacher at Barker College in Sydney. Teaching has taken her far and wide; from Newcastle, Raymond Terrace, The Entrance and Teacher Education at Macquarie University. Poetry is her "quiet passion". Lyn champions journal writing with her students and encourages poetic inclusions to stimulate the imagination.

LORISSE BAZLEY grew up in Lake Macquarie and now lives in Western Sydney. She is a devoted mother and student at Avondale College of Higher Education. With plenty on her plate, she takes great but seldom pleasure in little escapes to the beach for revitalisation.

JUDITH BEVERIDGE'S seventh collection of poems *Sun Music: New and Selected Poems* was published in 2018. She is the recipient of the Philip Hodgins Memorial Medal and the Christopher Brennan Award for lifetime achievement in poetry. She was poetry editor of *Meanjin* from 2002-2015, co-editor of the anthology *Contemporary Australian Poetry* and has been a teacher of poetry at the University of Sydney for many years. She lives in Sydney.

PETER BOYLE is a Sydney-based poet and translator of poetry. He is the author of seven books of poetry, most recently *Ghostspeaking* which won the 2017 Kenneth Slessor Prize and was shortlisted for the Adelaide Festival Award for Poetry. In 2017 he was also awarded the Philip Hodgins Memorial Medal for Excellence in Literature. As a translator of poetry from Spanish and French he has had seven books published, including *Three Poets from Argentina and Uruguay* (Vagabond Press, 2017), and *Índole/Of Such A Nature* by José Kozer (University of Alabama Press, 2018).

ANN CAMPBELL was born the middle-child of a family of seven. She trained and worked as a nurse until her children finished their education. Ann then completed her degree in counselling and works on the Chaplaincy team at Sydney Adventist Hospital. While grandmothering is a treasured part of her retirement, she also volunteers for projects such as the New Leaves poetry workshop.

KAYLA CARTER is studying Communications at Avondale College of Higher Education. Originally from Taupo, New Zealand, she abandoned home and country for warmer shores in 2016 and now lives in Cooranbong, NSW with her husband, Steve, and various house plants. Her hopes for the future include writing a novel and international travel.

EILEEN CHONG is a Sydney poet who was born in Singapore. She is the author of six books, the most recent being *Rainforest*, from Pitt Street Poetry. Individual poems of hers have shortlisted for the Newcastle Poetry Prize, the University of Canberra's Vice-Chancellor's Literary Awards, and twice for the Peter Porter Poetry Prize. Her books have shortlisted for the Anne Elder Award, the Victorian Premier's Literary Award, and twice for the Prime Minister's Literary Awards. www.eileenchong.com.au

LINDA CIRIC is a Bachelor of Arts student at Avondale College of Higher Education. With a major in International Poverty and Development Studies, she is passionate about social justice and advocating for the needs of the vulnerable and those at-risk. Her minors in Graphics Design and Communications allow her creative brain to bloom.

KERRYN COOMBS-VALEONTIS is a Sydney Based Art Therapist, Ecotherapist, and group facilitator, working in mental health. She currently lives in a caravan in the bush shared with all manner of wildlife and they often find their way into her poems.

LUCY DOUGAN's books include *White Clay* (Giramondo), *Meanderthals* (Web del Sol) and *The Guardians* (Giramondo). She has been published in a range of journals both here and overseas, and has had work represented in many anthologies. She has worked in arts administration, as a tertiary teacher of creative writing, literature and film, and as poetry editor of *HEAT* magazine and *Axon: Creative Explorations*. She currently works as Program Director for the China-Australia Writing Centre at Curtin. Her PhD, concerning representation of Naples, was awarded in 2010. *The Guardians* won the WA Premier's Prize for Poetry in 2016. In 2017 she co-edited *The Collected Poems of Fay Zwicky* (UWAP) with Tim Dolin.

STEPHEN EDGAR'S most recent book is *Transparencies* (Black Pepper Publishing, 2017). His two previous books, *Eldershaw* and *Exhibits of the Sun*, were both shortlisted for the Prime Minister's Literary Awards. His website can be found at <stephenedgar.com. au>.

BROOK EMERY'S first three books of poetry were *and dug my fingers in the sand* (FIP, 2000), which won the Judith Wright Calanthe Prize in the Queensland Premier's Literary Awards, *Misplaced Heart* (FIP, 2003) and *Uncommon Light* (FIP, 2007). All three were short-listed for the Kenneth Slessor Prize in the NSW Premier's Literary Awards. His fourth book, *Collusion* (John Leonard Press, 2012) was short-listed for the Western Australian Premier's Prize. He was born in 1949 and lives in Sydney.

JANE FERNANDEZ is Vice-President (Quality & Strategy) at *Avondale College of Higher Education*. Jane is also founding convenor of the *Higher Education Private Provider Quality Network* (HEPP-QN). Jane's interest is in leadership in higher education quality and practice. Jane is committed to developing and extending the quality foot-print of private higher education nationally in Australia and develops and leads quality projects to support this vision. Her academic background is in postcolonial literature. Her research interests include institutional quality assurance as well as postcolonial literary criticism.

JOHN FOULCHER has published eleven books of poetry, the most recent being *101 Poems* (Pitt Street Poetry 2016), a selection of work from his previous books, and *A Casual Penance* (PSP 2017). In 2010 he was the Literature Board of the Australia Council's resident at the Keesing Studio in Paris, an experience which resulted in his 2011 volume, *The Sunset Assumption*. He was a teacher in schools in NSW, the ACT and Victoria for nearly forty years; it was a vocation he loved. He lives in Canberra, and is at present working on his next book of poetry, tentatively titled *Collect*.

KATHRYN FRY has poems published in *Australian Love Poems* (2013), *A Slow Combusting Hymn* (2014), *Watermark* (2014), *Home is the Hunter* (2016), *ear to earth* (2017) and the Newcastle Poetry Prize anthologies of 2014 and 2016. Her poems are also in *Plumwood Mountain Journal* (2016), *Antipodes* (2016), *Cordite Poetry Review* (2016) and *Not Very Quiet* (2017, 2018). Her collection, *Green Point Bearings*, was published by Ginninderra Press in 2018.

HAYLEY GABRIELLE is a Melbourne-based writer with a keen interest in poetry, fantasy and science fiction. With a background in film and television, Hayley has pursued her writing ventures relentlessly, publishing poetry and short fiction across a range of journals and anthologies worldwide. *Essence*—a young adult fantasy novel—paves the way for her longer works.

EMMERSON ROSE GREY is a Second-Year Communications student from Monto, Queensland studying at Avondale College of Higher Education with the prospects of becoming a full-time public speaker. She is currently co-editing the on-campus publication *The Voice* and is the Lead Designer for Avondale's yearbook *The Jacaranda*. In her non-existent spare time, she enjoys creating art, adventuring, and discovering gems in the forms of underrated music.

ALTHEA HALLIDAY is a former Senior English teacher at Barker College, Hornsby. Her creative compositions have long been inspired by Dylan Thomas' exhortation to "love the words", and throughout her career, she encouraged her students to live their own story, and write their own verse.

DANIEL IONITA was born in Bucharest, Romania and teaches Organisational Improvement at the University of Technology Sydney. Published works include *Testament – Anthology of Romanian Verse,* the first comprehensive collection of Romanian poetry in English, *The Bessarabia of My Soul,* a representation, also in English, of poets from the Republic of Moldova, and three volumes of poetry, *Hanging between the Stars, ContraDiction* and *The Island of Words from Home.*

LINDA IRELAND has had work published in several Hunter anthologies, including *A Slow Combusting Hymn* (ASM and Cerberus Press 2014). For the last 3 years she has been a Community Teaching Assistant with ModPo, an international online course on modern American run out of the University of Pennsylvania. A member of BLUE Room Poets, Linda has helped establish Poetry in the Pub in Western Lake Macquarie.

JUDY JOHNSON has published eight books of poetry. She won the Victorian Premier's Award for poetry in 2007 and has been shortlisted in the WA and NSW Premier's awards. Her verse novel *Jack* was on the syllabus at both Melbourne and Sydney University.

SUE JOSEPH — A journalist for more than thirty five years, working in Australia and the UK, Sue Joseph (PhD) began working as an academic, teaching print journalism at the University of Technology Sydney in 1997. As a Senior Lecturer, she now teaches journalism and creative writing, particularly creative non-fiction writing, in both undergraduate and postgraduate programs. Her research interests are around sexuality, secrets and confession, framed by the media; ethics and trauma narrative; memoir; reflective professional practice; ethical HDR supervision; nonfiction poetry; and Australian creative non-fiction. Her fourth book, *Behind the Text: Candid conversations with Australian creative nonfiction writers,* was released in 2016. She is currently Reviews Editor of *Ethical Space: The International Journal of Communication Ethics.*

CHRISTOPHER (KIT) KELEN has a dozen full length collections in English as well as translated in Chinese, Portuguese, French, Italian, Spanish, Indonesian, Swedish and Filipino. His next volume of poetry is *Poor Man's Coat — Hardanger Poems*, to be published by UWAP in 2018. In 2017, Kit was shortlisted twice for the Montreal Poetry Prize and won the Local Award in the Newcastle Poetry Prize. Emeritus Professor at the University of Macau, in 2017, Kit Kelen was awarded an honorary doctorate by the University of Malmö, in Sweden.

BELINDA KENT had her first success as a writer at fifteen when she had her first short story published. Since then she has continued writing sporadically amidst the calamity of study, work and, of course, travel. She loves drawing inspiration from her own experiences and those common to the everyday human existence. She is in her fourth year of a Bachelor of Arts/Bachelor of Teaching (Secondary) degree majoring in English, and hopes to continue her own writing of both prose and poetry as she cultivates a love for such works in her students in the future.

JEAN KENT grew up in rural Queensland and now lives at Lake Macquarie. She has published five full-length poetry collections. Her most recent books are *The Hour of Silvered Mullet* (Pitt Street Poetry, 2015) and *Paris in my Pocket* (PSP, 2016), a selection of her poems from an Australia Council residency in Paris. With Kit Kelen, in 2014 Jean co-edited *A Slow Combusting Hymn: Poetry from and about Newcastle and the Hunter Region*. Samples of her poems and occasional jottings are on her website http://jeankent.net/

ANDY KISSANE has published a novel, a book of short stories, *The Swarm*, and four books of poetry. *Radiance* (Puncher & Wattmann, 2014) was shortlisted for the Victorian and Western Australian Premier's Prizes and the Adelaide Festival Awards. He was the winner of the 2017 Tom Collins Prize for Poetry. http://andykissane.com

ESTELLE KNIGHT has called the Gold Coast home for much of her life. Her love for words has been passed down from her grandmother, who crafted together an "itty bitty book" full of sayings and quotes which she still treasures today. Estelle is currently in her second year of Bachelor of Arts/Bachelor of Teaching (Secondary) with a major in English. She is looking forward to a future in education and hopes to develop within her students an appreciation for the power of language.

RICHARD LANDER is retired and commenced writing poetry as a form of therapy after being diagnosed with prostate cancer in 2007. He is married to Lyndall and lives in Sydney. Some of Richard's other poetry has been published in *The New Leaves Poetry Anthology*, *Wording the World*, and *Here not there*.

MARTIN LANGFORD has published seven books of poetry, the most recent of which is *Ground* (P&W, 2015). He is co-editor (with J. Beveridge, J. Johnson and D. Musgrave) of *Contemporary Australian Poetry* (Puncher & Wattmann, 2016). An essayist and critic, he is the poetry reviewer for *Meanjin*.

LYNNETTE LOUNSBURY is a writer, lecturer, coffee-drinker, fighter, baller, dog-walker, candle-maker, pop culturalist, poet, handy-girl, traveller, filmmaker, mother of dragons, gardener, cosplayer and beatnik. She is the author of *We Ate the Road Like Vultures* (Inkerman & Blunt) and is reasonably well prepared for an apocalypse.

WIN LUBEN is a retired nurse living in Sydney who has a keen interest in learning about other cultures. Over the years she has enjoyed gardening and conversations with her Dog. She keeps her mind active with new activities like poetry writing, and some of her poems have been previously published in *The New Leaves Poetry Anthology*, *Wording the World*, and *Here not there*.

CHRISTIAN McCLELLAND has, for as long as he can remember, been incredibly fascinated by the exploration of the world, be it through reading and writing, science, or travel. Perhaps his earliest memory is of looking at a towering bookshelf and being entranced by curiosity. Chris is currently pursuing a Bachelor of Secondary Education with an English major and hopes his love of words will catch on.

GREG MCLAREN'S most recent books include *Australian ravens* (Puncher & Wattmann), *After Han Shan* (Flying Islands) and *The Kurri Kurri Book of the Dead* (Puncher & Wattmann). *Windfall* (Puncher & Wattmann) is due in late 2018. He lives in the lower Blue Mountains with his partner and daughter, and is a poet, critic and teacher. McLaren's work has been almost widely anthologised. His poems appear in *Windchimes: Asia in Australian Poetry* (ed. by Noel Rowe and Vivian Smith), *Australian Poetry from 1788* (ed. by Robert Gray and Geoffrey Lehmann), *A Slow Combusting Hymn: Poetry from and about Newcastle and the Hunter Region* (ed. by Kit Kelen and Jean Kent), and in *Contemporary Australian Poetry* (ed. by Martin Langford, Judith Beveridge, Judy Johnson and David Musgrave).

ANIA MITCHELL was born in Mildura, Victoria, but currently calls Queensland's Sunshine Coast home. Studying a Bachelor of Arts/ Bachelor of Teaching (Secondary) with a major in English, it is safe to say that at any given time you will find her engrossed in some witty novel. She finds comfort in the poetry of Wisława Szymborska, and wishes the Ancient Library of Alexandria had never burned down . . .

BETHANY MORROW is studying a Bachelor of Arts with a double major in International Poverty and Development Studies and Communications. She is inspired by poetry that can capture people with the beauty of the natural world.

DAVID MUSGRAVE is the author of the novel, *Glissando: a Melodrama*. His latest collection of poetry is *Anatomy of Voice*, GloriaSMH 2016. He runs the publishing company Puncher & Wattmann and lectures in creative writing at the University of Newcastle. He has won numerous awards for his poetry.

SAMANTHA NIGHTINGALE wrote her first poem at age 7, it went like this: "The trees, the trees have leaves." Needless to say she has come a long way. Having completed a Bachelor of Psychological Science, she is now working her way through a double degree – a Bachelor of Teaching and a Bachelor of Arts with a major in English. Samantha considers herself an avid reader and an occasional poet.

CARA ONTANU is a creative at heart who embraces many expressions of art – ranging from painting and writing to her impressive skill in procrastination. Currently completing her final year in counselling at Avondale College of Higher Education, she hopes to continue further into ministry and pursue her passion for working with young people. Cara admires a healthy lifestyle but is still battling her love for cheese or cookie-cream ice-cream.

JAN OWEN'S seventh book of verse, *The Offhand Angel*, was published in 2015 and her translations from Baudelaire's *Les Fleurs du Mal* came out with Arc Publications in the same year. In 2016 she received the Philip Hodgins Memorial Medal and the following year was awarded the Multicultural NSW Early Career Translator Prize.

DONNA PINTER is a designer, educator, fine art photographer, amateur poet, wife to Dean and mother to two beautiful girls Ruby and Coco. In addition to owning boutique graphic Design firm, satellite ink, Donna has lectured in Graphic Design at Avondale College since 2004. Always creatively pursuing her heart's path by fearlessly making marks with design, photography, typography, colour, conversation, paint and the written word.

MELANIE REYES is an enthusiastic reader of modern-day literature. She plans on one day publishing a novel of her own, to use as a conversation starter. She is currently in her last year of her degree in Education, majoring in English and minoring in Modern History. She is fiercely loved and supported by her family, inspired by the coasts of Western Australia, and always leaves two minutes aside for the culinary delight of noodles.

CAROLYN RICKETT is an Associate Dean (Research), Senior Lecturer in Communication, and creative arts practitioner at Avondale College of Higher Education. Her research and teaching interests focus on: pedagogy and practice, trauma and bereavement studies; writing as therapeutic intervention; memoir and autobiographical writing; medical humanities; journalism ethics and praxis; literary and poetry studies; chaplaincy, and the psychosocial and spiritual care of patients. She is one of the research leaders at Avondale College's Lifestyle Research Centre and serves on the board for the Christian Education Research Centre. Carolyn is also a chaplain on the Spiritual Care Services team at Sydney Adventist Hospital.

RAY ROENNFELDT has been President of Avondale College of Higher Education since 2009. "Seeing Deep" is his first attempt at poetry. He regrets that he has probably left his run too late to become a world-famous poet!

PAT SAAR was born in Melbourne and trained as a nurse before moving to Sydney, bringing up her family and working in the operating theatres. Thirty years later, she attended university to up-grade her qualifications. She is at present retired, widowed and went back to university to complete a history degree. She has also completed her first novel.

JEFFERSON SHAW grew up in Sydney NSW, and moved to the Central Coast in 2016 to study a Bachelor of Arts at Avondale College. During his time there he has written multiple articles for a student magazine and the college's yearbook, *The Jac*. After gaining experience with his writing, he became the lead writer for the 2018 edition of *The Jac*. He hopes to continue his writing in novels and poetry, and further develop skills in areas of the media such as Film and Radio.

DALE SMEDLEY by day is a full time Bachelor of Arts student at Avondale College, where he is studying Counselling with a minor in Communications. At night (okay, also during the day) he transforms into a fulltime husband and dad, only distinguishable from the student by the subtraction of reading glasses. He is also a part time, musician, fisherman, writer, home chef, wrestling fan (yes he knows you are going to roll your eyes) and an avid conversationalist. Keen to expand his repertoire, he decided to explore the limits of his creative ability by signing up for a creative writing subject. He discovered through the exploration of the limits of his creativeness that there are no limits. He is keen to continue on the journey and discover the realms of imagination that are at his disposal.

TODD TURNER is an Australian poet who lives and works in Sydney. His debut collection of poetry *Woodsmoke* was published by Black Pepper Publishing in 2014. The book was shortlisted for the Dame Mary Gilmore Award and the Anne Elder Award. Turner's poems have been widely published in literary journals and newspapers such as *Meanjin, Southerly, Overland* and *The Australian.* His work features in anthologies such as *The Best Australian Poems* (Black Inc.) and *Contemporary Australian Poetry* (Puncher & Wattmann, 2016).

AMBER VINCENT is Coordinator of English and History at Macquarie College, Newcastle. She has taught English at all levels in New South Wales, and is a devotee of Ancient History. She is drawn to storytellers both past and present, and encourages her students to live and write deliberately.

Acknowledgements

Judith Beveridge's "Sugarcane Juice" and "Cobra" are from *Sun Music: New and Selected Poems*, Giramondo, 2018.

Eileen Chong's "Green Grief "was first published in *Spineless Wonders: Time* anthology, February 2018, Australia; "Dog Meals" was first published in *Voice and Verse Magazine*, April 2018, Hong Kong.

Lucy Dougan's "Looks" was previously published on the FAWWA website. "English Woman at the Palermo Cathedra" is unpublished.

Stephen Edgar's "Parallax" appeared in *Axon: Creative Explorations*; "Unminded" appeared in *Meanjin*.

Brook Emery's "Broken / Beautiful" and "But it would be loathsome stiff" were published in his last book *Have Been and Are* (Gloria SMH, 2016).

John Foulcher's "Reading Josephus" and "Innes Foulcher (1897 – 1984)" were first published in *Pictures from the War* (Angus & Robertson 1987).

Kathryn Fry's "The Bowen Mango" and "All the Willing Hours" are both from her collection *Green Point Bearings*, Ginnindera Press, 2018.

Linda Ireland's "Whale Fossil at Anatini NZ" was published in *A Slow Combusting Hymn: Poetry from and about Newcastle and the Hunter Region.* :"Worlds" was published in *Blue Room Poets Anthology 2*.

Judy Johnson's "White Potato Vine" and "Statice" were both published in: *counsel for the defence*, IPSI foundation, Canberra, 2016.

Christopher (Kit) Kelen's poems were shortlisted for the Montreal Poetry Prize, 2017.

Jean Kent's "Rue des Deux Ponts" was first published in *The Canberra Times*. "Sunday Kites" is from *Travelling with the Wrong Phrasebooks*, Pitt Street Poetry, 2012.

Andy Kissane's "The Last Quarter" was published in *Grieve: Stories and Poems about Grief and Loss*, Vol 5, Hunter Writers Centre, 2017. "A Personal History of Joy" was published in *Joy: 2017 ACU Prize for Poetry*, Australian Catholic University, 2017.

Jan Owen's "Aegina" was published in the UK in a 2017 festschrift for John Lucas: *Strike Up the Band*, edited by Merryn Williams, and "Tough Muscle" was published in *The Hippocrates Book of the Heart*, edited by Wendy French, Michael Hulse and Donald Singer, Hippocrates Press, 2017.

Carolyn Rickett's 'Sweet Peas' was published in *New Leaves Anthology*, Sydney: Darlington Press an imprint of Sydney University Press, 2008.

Carolyn Rickett's 'Waking' was published in J. Kent & K. Kelen (Eds.), *A slow combusting hymn: Poetry from and about the Newcastle and Hunter Region*, Markwell, Australia: Cerberus Press, 2014.

Todd Turner's "Horse" appeared in *The Weekend Australian Review*, 7-8 January, 2017. "The Stick" appeared in *The Weekend Australian Review*, 25-26 February, 2017.

Thank You

My heartiest thanks and congratulations to Dr Carolyn Rickett, Jean Kent, Dr David Musgrave, Donna Pinter and Margaret House for their leadership and management of the anthology project and to all students for your creative participation in this worthy project. My very special thanks to the established poets for your time and investment in inspiring and supporting our journey. Avondale is grateful for, and privileged by, your collaboration.

—Professor Jane Fernandez
Vice President (Quality & Strategy)
Avondale College of Higher Education